D1563619

SPAIN TRAVEL GUIDE 2022

Discover Top Sights, Hidden Gems, and Learn to Live Like the Locals

Explore to Win

TABLE OF CONTENTS

INTRODUCTION

Traveling across the world and exploring a new country can be both exciting and daunting. This guide is here to help you be prepared and informed about travel around Spain so that any concerns or confusion will be washed away. You deserve to experience the most out of your international trip with as much adventure and relaxation as possible. Your travels should be as stress-free as possible, and the chapters of this guide will provide you with the necessary travel tips and information to ensure that you have the best and most unique trip across the country of Spain. This guide is for all sorts of travelers and has been adapted for different needs, interests, and of course the protocols needed to be followed during the Covid-19 pandemic. We have got it all figured out so that you can follow suit with ease, because that is what a holiday is all about!

In Chapter 1, the practical steps to planning a trip will be discussed. Here, we will go through some methods you can follow to save time and money to avoid regrets or any complications when you are on holiday. Depending on your needs, timeline, and budget, this chapter will allow you to plan out your trip by sharing some travel tips and techniques you can apply when preparing for your trip before you even start. You need to dedicate time to plan out the logistics of your trip while also clarifying what your interests and expectations are, realistic or not, so that you can create a travel plan that works *for* you and not against you.

In Chapter 2, we will look at the many attractions you could visit on your trip to Spain. This chapter is dedicated to sharing the diversity of the country, as there are different attractions and places you could visit that offer different experiences. The places you visit should be about your interests and your unique sense of adventure. Therefore, we have compiled a list of must-see attractions, tourist-friendly places, as well as authentically Spanish hidden gems. Where you go and what you get out of your trip depend on you, but we are here to provide you with all the travel options you can choose as the possibilities are endless.

When you travel to another country with its own language and cultural norms, being knowledgeable about these different ways of living will only make your trip easier and much more invigorating. In Chapter 3, we give you tips and tricks to try out so that you can immerse yourself in Spanish culture. This means that connecting with the people you meet along the way will help you feel less lost and more settled, confident, and brave when you are visiting a foreign country. Therefore, in Chapter 3, we list some methods you can follow to connect with the culture through learning some Spanish, talking to locals, and adopting some Spanish ways of living.

To feel at ease in Spain, you need to take a breath, observe, and then just become part of the vibrant culture. Chapter 4 provides you with more ways to immerse yourself in the culture. This chapter discusses places and ways to eat and shop, different accommodations, and other Spanish activities that are inherent to the culture. Through food and drink, nightlife, and suburbs, you will be able to feel part of the country and be open to the gift of travel.

While traveling should be care-free, for the most part, we do have unforeseen and unquestionable restrictions due to the current Covid-19 pandemic. The rules and steps to protection and prevention are provided in Chapter 5. In Spain, like most countries, there are certain protocols one needs to follow when spending time in public places. Spain also has its own travel policies that need to be followed. Once you are aware of and follow protocol, you will be able to save time and energy when on holiday. Being prepared and informed before and during any trip at any time will always make for a more enjoyable and less stressful experience.

Lastly, in Chapter 6, we take a deep-dive into the geography of the country. This chapter offers different types of travelers the opportunity to choose their own path. The busy streets in cities or the quiet roads in the suburbs and villages are all there waiting for you to walk them. When on foot, you will have the time to soak up the scenery, the scents, and the sounds of Spain. That is why becoming your own tour guide through the streets of Spain is another opportunity to become even more immersed in the country's culture and all the special gifts it has to offer you. We will look at the maps, roads, towns, villages, and even islands that you can visit in and around Spain. This chapter gives you the roadmap to the perfect Spanish holiday, including must-see places, the unheard-of villages, the lively cities, and the tranquil beaches and islands. This chapter showcases the diverse landscape of Spain that is all available for you to explore. Spain is waiting for you along with all of the precious memories you will make on your trip!

CHAPTER 1:

PREPARE FOR YOUR BEST HOLIDAY

Plan Your Trip and Timeline

When on holiday, we tend to not follow our usual routine. We eat at different hours and spend our days doing activities we would not usually do. It can almost seem like we lose track of time. Well, sometimes we do when we are jet-lagged, but other times we get lost in the excitement of the endless possibilities when on holiday. There are so many choices and so much to do when you are in a foreign country, especially when you are visiting for the first time. This situation can cause us to not think clearly and become overwhelmed or even just go with the flow without taking time to think things through. We are here to help you learn to stop and take a moment to create a timeline and not leave Spain with regrets or any "should haves."

Time-Saving Tips

Time is precious when you are in a foreign country because you want to experience so many new things and see all that the country has to offer in a specific, usually quite limited, amount of time. This means you need to know your timeline and always remind yourself of the length of your stay. If you are on a two-week holiday, you cannot expect to travel to all the different towns and cities in Spain. It is an entire country, and traveling across the country will not give you the opportunity to truly enjoy any one specific moment or even stop to relax. When planning your timeline for your holiday, you need to be realistic and remain honest with yourself. Your timeline will need to be planned out in a way that gives you enough time to do the activities *you* want to do in a specific amount of time. You will not be able to experience everything, but you can experience everything you came to experience. This means, you need to plan out each day and allocate a must-do activity per day that follows your unique desires and travel dreams.

Once you have a better understanding of what you want to experience on your holiday, you need to factor in travel time as different places could be far from one another, and modes of transport differ in travel time, distance, and the number of stops, routes, and schedules. It's also wise to factor in some time to do nothing—when you free up time or even entire days to just relax and recharge for your next adventure. Again, you can decide what you want out of your holiday and how your trip will unfold based on your unique interests, which will allow you to plan and then live out your holiday dreams!

Below is a list of factors you need to consider when creating your holiday timeline and planner:

- The length of your stay
- Your budget
- Your activity wishlist
- Your travel group or companions
- Your location
- Your mode of transport
- Your accommodation

We've compiled a list of smart time-saving tips for you that will equip you for your trip and ensure you don't feel the need to rush to the next adventure because of fear of missing out:

- Do your research beforehand. When you are planning an international trip, you need to be informed about the country and your particular travel goals. This includes looking at the best flights that suit your needs as well as any extra documentation or logistical factors. You can save time by planning all you possibly can before you even step foot on your flight to Spain. Booking a return flight, your accommodation, some guided tours, and sorting out any travel documents you might need can all be done beforehand. The more time you spend planning, researching, and organizing before your trip will mean that you will spend less time doing admin during your trip, making it an easier and smoother experience. Knowing about all the traveling requirements you need to meet and then checking these boxes will help make your actual trip less stressful and give you more time to actually *be* on holiday.

- Make use of apps and travel sites. When planning before your holiday, or even during your holiday, you can make use of accommodation or site-seeing websites. These can be local or international websites that will allow you to book trips and accommodation before you arrive at your destination. These apps often offer promotions and share essential information like trading hours or pricing. You can also download transport and delivery apps on your cell phone that can make it easier for you to get to places or eat in while being set up for your unique needs and preferences.

- Make reservations. Again, this can save you time because you will not need to be waiting in long lines at tourist hotspots, restaurants, parks, museum tours, and so many other places only to find out that you need to book beforehand or that the place is already fully booked. You can waste a lot of time waiting for *potential* activities at places. Going online or calling the institution to make a reservation beforehand will ensure that you won't waste time and money traveling to places only to wait in a line outside.

- Create a rough routine for each day. When you know what Spain has to offer and what your interests are, you can implement a daily plan to do all the things that are on your Spanish holiday wishlist. Once you have a list of all the activities and places you want to experience on your trip, you can then work around these to create a tentative routine. This means, your beach trip or your trip to an island will affect your meals and outfits as well as money and time spent on transport. Knowing what you want to do and where you want to go will allow you to adjust your day-to-day chores and activities to make room for the items on your holiday wish list that need to be ticked off before leaving the country.

- Map out your travel routes. Getting lost in a foreign country can be stressful and waste a lot of time and unforeseen spending. Knowing where you are going and how to get there before you leave your accommodation is essential. Unless you are dedicating the day to wandering the cobbled streets of Spain, you will need to follow a map to get to your destination. Being informed about travel time, potential traffic, and parking areas are a plus. Ordering a driving service or taking public transport routes with locals, in addition to having a map, can also be a support as locals can offer help and directions. Knowing where you are going and how to get there before you go on your way will make a much easier commute.

- Avoid busy tourist hotspots. These places can be flooded with people, which can mean long lines just to get into a place. Getting anything done at a place that is busy or where servers have their hands full will take more than double the time. You will be using most of your holiday time just waiting on getting service, waiting in line, and walking slower in busy places due to large crowds. This can all be very frustrating and take the fun out of any experience as well as essential time out of your holiday.

- Learn common and useful phrases. Knowing some Spanish phrases and words can help you throughout your trip to avoid getting lost in many towns and cities. Being stuck in a situation where there has been miscommuni-cation can definitely take up time. Getting lost due to a misunderstanding of directions or struggling to shop at a local market because you cannot ask for the price of something can lead to seconds and then minutes wasted each day. Using a few Spanish phrases for your everyday activities can make your communication and expeditions around Spain so much easier!

Create a Budget and Stick to It!

Budget Tips and Money-Wise Travel Hacks

- Create a daily budget. Some people can go on holiday and have the privilege of not having to even think about their bills, but others (like most of us) need to ensure they don't spend money they can't really spend or just don't have. If you fall under the latter, you need to know how important it is to create a daily budget that is modest but flexible. Observe your Spanish holiday lifestyle and know your interests, needs, and holiday wishlist. Once you have an idea of what you will be spending your money on, you can allocate your spending money to these things. You can divide your holiday spending money by the days that you will be in Spain. This budget needs to include your transport, food, recreation, accommodation, and miscellaneous things like treats, unforeseen costs, or gifts for your loved ones back home. Again, knowing what you want out of your holiday as well as what Spain has to offer before you begin your travels will help you get a clear idea of your holiday budget as you will know what things cost in this country.

- Eat in or go grocery shopping. Dining out at a restaurant can be expensive. Some establishments are pricier than others, and most are more expensive than a bag of groceries from the local supermarket. Shopping like locals can save you so much money. Not only can you buy in bulk and get more for your money, but you can also buy groceries and snacks that will last longer. Depending on your accommodation, you can buy groceries for a few days and store them in a mini refrigerator or in a kitchen/ kitchenette. You can pack lunches to take with you on trips instead of spending money on convenience items or restaurant prices.

- Look for deals or sales. This is an international golden rule: Buying on sale costs less money than buying at the original price. This doesn't always mean that the item is better; in some cases, you could be buying an item that is expired or damaged. You need to be wise about buying items on sale. Certain deals could be beneficial, but make sure you don't spend money on a deal that you don't really need or want. This is just impulsive buying and isn't wise when trying to save money. Again, it's important to know what you need and want and *then* look out for deals and sales that are worth it; this helps you avoid spending money on necessities like food and rather have extra money for more unique adventures. You need to remember that your spending depends on your personal priorities and how *you* want to spend your money and time when on holiday.

- Walk instead of drive. Renting a car is convenient, but most services or items that make your life convenient are usually more costly. Therefore, depending on your budget and timeline, you could try to walk to local hotspots like stores, landmarks, markets, restaurants, beaches, bars, etc. This also depends on the location of your accommodation. Sometimes, spending a bit more money on your accommodation that is centrally located can save you time and money in the long run. Living close to the places you would like to visit will allow you to walk around or take short trips by public transport, which is much more affordable than personal taxi services, rental cars, or long-distance train rides.

- Look for places with free Wi-Fi or get a local SIM card. Using your cellphone as it is can either mean additional costs or zero phone service. Relying on Wi-Fi can also be a problem when you are constantly up and down, moving from place to place. While Wi-Fi is almost everywhere in Spain, like most countries, institutions will require you to be a guest or customer in order for you to use their Wi-Fi and some public Wi-Fi is not always safe. Getting a local SIM card can help you receive cost-effective mobile services without any hassle or unnecessary international fees involved. You can also pay as you use these services and monitor your data usage whenever you are not using Wi-Fi.

- Follow the locals. Tourist hotspots are usually overpriced in most countries, meaning you can find yourself spending unnecessary money on a traditional Spanish dish that could be half the price at a more authentic local restaurant. You might even be surprised at how fresh, tasty, and even better some meals are at local and smaller restaurants compared to expensive, tourist-attracting restaurants.

- Avoid ordering water. Instead, stock up on store-bought water and refill your own personal water bottle to stay hydrated throughout the day. Ordering a bottle of still or sparkling water at a restaurant will be much more expensive than a bottle you bought at the store. Buying in bulk is better as you get even more for your money. Therefore, buying a container of liters of water and decanting it into your water bottle is the most budget-friendly way to keep yourself hydrated while you are walking up and down the city. Unless you're only staying in the city of Madrid with high-quality tap water, you should always carry a bottle of distilled water with you as you travel across the country, as not all regions have drinkable tap water.

- Remain flexible. This may seem counterintuitive, but it is not the case. To save time, money, and energy, you need to leave room for some adjustments. By not being fixated on a certain date and time, and rather being flexible with your holiday plans, you could save yourself so much money. Prices for most tourist activities range due to peak times and dates. You can save money by adjusting your dates for certain trips to suit your pocket and not sticking to your initial expectation of doing activities on one specific day. Remaining open can give you the opportunity to find bargains when it comes to day trips, rides, and even eating out. For instance, you may have wanted to eat out on a Saturday night, but changing that to a Monday night with a 50% off special will save you money while enjoying the same meal. You can get the same experience of eating out, going on a cruise, or even staying at a beachfront hotel if you are willing to be more flexible with your time and keep your expectations to a minimum. Being a traveler requires thinking on your feet and enjoying what the country has to offer with an open mind.

CHAPTER 2:

DISCOVER THE TOP SIGHTS AND HIDDEN GEMS

Must-See Places and Spaces

Tourist Attractions for Everyone

Below is a list of tourist attractions for every type of traveler, from single adventurers to family groups:

- Sagrada Família—an iconic masterpiece designed by architect Antoni Gaudí and located in Barcelona. This Roman Catholic church, known as the "Church of the Sacred Family," is unique in every way and construction dates back to 1882. Although unfinished and still under construction, the building is breathtaking inside and outside, with its many spires and stained glass windows. This church is one of the most visited attractions in Spain, making it a UNESCO World Heritage site. Tip: Buy your tickets online before you plan to visit, as this is one of the most popular attractions in the city of Barcelona and attracts about three million visitors each year.

- Plaza Mayor—the center of Spanish life in the capital city, Madrid. This plaza has been part of city and community life since the 16th century with ceremonies, entertainment, and events like bullfights all taking place here. Designed by Juan de Herrera, this plaza has stood the test of time. It is still very much a hub for people to come together and experience the wonders of Spanish culture, from cafes to shaded world-class restaurants. People can connect from all over the world. The traditional Spanish market, known as San Miguel Market, is located close to the plaza to enjoy more affordable tapas and beverages.

- Güell Park—a creation by Antoni Gaudí that serves as a wonderful park in the Gràcia district of Barcelona. Known as Parc Güell, this is yet another example of the artistic genius of Gaudí as it is bright in color and diverse in texture with mosaic designs across the park. This attraction is great to visit for an afternoon stroll with an easy and carefree approach to walking through the park, giving yourself time to soak in all the magic that this attraction has to offer. This park is also a great place for a family outing as you can enjoy the fresh, warm air of Spain while admiring the rainbows of fun color provided by the designer in an open space of possibility.

- Santiago de Compostela—an attraction holding the cathedral that is the burial site of St. James as well as the endpoint of the pilgrimage known as the Camino de Santiago. This site is rich in history, especially the history of the church and its connection to the Old Town. The cathedral was completed in 1211 and exhibits features of Roman and Spanish architecture seen in the high-rise bell towers. While the cathedral is the heart of the Old Town, this site is perfect for a walk into the past with its charm, art, restaurants, and historic and newer streets with the bustle of tourists and students. Tip: Go on the rooftop tour to experience the magnificent views of the old world provided by Santiago de Compostela.

- The Guggenheim Museum Bilbao — an iconic art museum designed by architect Frank Gehry. Built in 1997, this building is iconic as it stands out from the rest of Spanish architecture, with its unique design recognizable by its gigantic glass and titanium sheets from its exterior. Located in Bilbao, this museum provides the city with postmodern architecture while holding contemporary art exhibits from Spain as well as from countries all over the world. The Guggenheim Museum not only showcases the art of its exhibits, but it also highlights the diversity of art and culture in the country of Spain. If you are an art lover or just appreciate the diversity of architecture in Spain, visit the Guggenheim Museum in Bilbao.

- Alcázar — a UNESCO World Heritage Site located in the center of Seville. This is a construction near the grand Seville cathedral, with a Moorish palace and remarkable gardens. The gardens are filled with many flowers, old palm trees, and elegant arches. The palace is now used by the Spanish Royal Family and holds so much history and unique features inherent to its time and style, like an underground bathhouse, while also offering a blend of Christian and Islamic finishings and furnishing. The many unique, intricate, and multi-national aspects of this site make it what it is—it is a place that should be on your must-see list. Not only does it have a connection to many eras and cultures, it was also a location for the award-winning series, *Game of Thrones*. Whether you are a fan of art becoming life or just an admirer of the beauty that comes out of history, you would appreciate what Alcázar has to offer.

- The Great Mosque of Cordoba—known as Mezquita of Cordoba, with *mezquita* being the Spanish word for 'mosque'—is a wondrous form of art and spirituality. With its design and features originating from a timeline of merging of cultures from Roman, Visigothic, then Moorish inspiration, this mosque is a delightful exhibition of the beauty seen in a collage of cultures that history allows. The many religious purposes of this sight make it a must-see historical attraction as well as a display of pure art with its marble floors, arches, columns, bright mosaics, and many unique design features that you can't find in any other place.

- Alhambra—a must-see palace situated in the city of Granada. This palace is hard to miss as it is a place that is of the old Moorish world of kings and grand structures. Not only is the Alhambra pleasing to observe, but the surrounding area also offers many tourist-friendly activities. These include lookout points of tranquility or tourist-filled spots of vendors and buskers. The nightlife and establishments in and around the area make it perfect for tourists to admire the uniquely Spanish structure while also enjoying the activities that you should relish in when on holiday in a foreign and high-energy country.

- Basílica de Santa María la Real de Covadonga— the iconic pink church in the National Park of Picos de Europa mountain range. This church is an architectural beauty as it is built from pink limestone, making it stand out from all the greenery that surrounds it. There are many sights to see in its vicinity like a beautiful waterfall and the glacial lakes, Lake Enol and

Lake Ercina. This area, with its natural beauty, is perfectly contrasted with the bright grand building that towers over all the land.

Hidden Gems to Discover

Local Treasures

Spain offers a wide range of activities and authentic traditions. If you are wanting a more local trip without all the hustle and bustle of tourist hotspots, there are many culturally-rich or remote places to experience. Here is a list of places to try out if you are an avid or curious traveler who prefers to go off the beaten track:

- Avila — a medieval town with charm and walls of great design and centuries of history. This town is made up of quiet, archaic streets as well as busy nightlife. Avila can seem like a one-dimensional town with its well-known walls, but it also has so much more to offer. After admiring the architecture of the town, you can enjoy the many local foods and festivities. With streets lined with small specialty shops and bars, as well as galleries and museums, this town provides so much Spanish culture that has transcended the medieval era to today's modern amenities and designs.
- Las Médulas — a natural beauty created by past human activity found in Provincia de León. With bright, contrasting colors, this range of hills and valleys is the result of ancient technologies that involved hydraulic power to exploit gold deposits. The site was once seen as a complex channel system with running water that moved through tunnels and lakes. The system has left the area with its distinctive, reddish, clay-like appearance that stands out next to the green of the flora that has now grown over it. If you are interested in natural beauties and ancient technologies, or just a perfect aesthetically pleasing social media

setting, then Las Médulas is a place to admire on your journey through Spain.

- Palace of Catalan Music—a palace for the history of classical music in Barcelona. This palace is a museum that honors music, like that of the great composers, Rachmaninov or Prokofiev. Not only does this palace hold so much history and innovation of the arts, it is also a glory of architectural design with its high beamed ceilings and stucco creations. The palace, like so many sights in Spain, is a building that serves its purpose as a place to preserve history as well as design.

- Ronda and its Gorge—this quaint village in the Spanish mountains dates back to the 9th century. Being one of the oldest towns in the country, there is so much human history to admire, but there is also so much natural beauty. The gorge that splits the village of Ronda is a sight that should not be missed if you are ever in the area. The gorge of Ronda is a photographer's dream as it makes an amazing photo-ready scene. There is also the Puente Nuevo bridge that allows one to walk across the gorge, adding to the wow-factor of this experience in the natural and quaint setting of Ronda.

- Extremadura's Valle del Jerte—a place to witness the bloom of cherry blossoms. The Jerte Valley is an art piece created by nature every single spring. Yes, Spain, too, has a season of cherry blossoms. If you are happy to visit the country in spring, you just might be in luck to witness the 15 days of cherry blossoms blooming in the valley near Cáceres. You can make a plan to travel to the valley between late March to early April to experience the cherry blossom season that is unique to Spain. While this is a special attraction, it may get busy as it only occurs once a year, so many people may come from all parts of Spain to be in the valley at the same time. There is no need to worry, as the trip to the expansive valley is worth it; it is a chance to walk through a wide valley covered in white flowers surrounding your feet with every step.

- Sant Pau Art Nouveau Site—a modernist creation other than Gaudí. There are many buildings across the country of Spain that showcase the vibrancy of its architecture and authentic flair, specifically in the city of Barcelona. Not far from the tourist favorite, Sagrada Família, there stands the Sant Pau Nouveau Site, a building by the architect Lluís

Doménech i Monataner. The building used to be a hospital but now is an expression of true Spanish modernist architecture. Tip: If you enjoy Spanish modernist architecture, outside the scope of Gaudí, you can go on a hunt for creations across Barcelona—an architectural art scavenger hunt. You can admire Casaramona, the work of Puig i Cadafalch, which used to serve as a yarn and textile factory and is now one of Barcelona's best art museums known as the Caixaforum.

- Picos de Europa—this is a national park located in the North of Spain. With its isolated and picturesque landscape, this site is great for anyone wanting to enjoy the true natural beauty of Spain without the crowds and typical tourist activities. Here, you can stop and walk along the trails and look out for the local animals. This park is great for outdoor group or family trips as it doesn't require spending money on overpriced entry fees or wasting time in long lines. Instead, you can walk at your own leisure and enjoy the peace and freedom of what the Spanish countryside has to offer as you hike, mountain climb, and even kayak in the fresh outdoors!

CHAPTER 3:

CONNECT WITH THE LOCAL CULTURE

Learn the Language and Study the Culture

As you travel across cities and meet people from different parts of the world, you will soon realize that language is a part of a culture—it carries culture in everyday life. The Spanish language reveals so much about Spanish culture because it's part of the reason why a distinct Spanish culture exists. When you start to observe and listen to people speaking and communicating with each other, you will see how the language is used and how it plays a role in the distinct lifestyle of Spain. Therefore, learning some Spanish phrases and words will not only help you get by in the country, but it will also open the door to becoming part of the unique way of life. Learning to connect with the country and its people through their own language will allow you to have a richer experience when visiting Spain.

You may not know a single word of Spanish, or maybe you've forgotten the Spanish you learned in school. There is no need to worry — you don't need to be fluent in the language to start to feel connected to the culture. Here are a few ways you can improve your Spanish language learning:

- Get a book or guide of Spanish phrases and study it before your trip to Spain.
- Watch Spanish movies or series to expose yourself to how the language sounds before your trip.
- Listen to Spanish music; it's so vibrant and romantic that it's impossible to not enjoy it.
- Practice speaking some words and phrases to improve your pronunciation.
- Make a local friend who is bilingual when in Spain to ease you into the Spanish language.
- Go to local hotspots like restaurants, parks, stores, etc. and be intentional about not only going to tourist-friendly places or cities where most people speak English.
- Don't be scared to use what you have learned in a real-life situation, so try to order your meal or ask for directions in Spanish.

Connect With Local People and Communities

Another way to experience a more authentic Spanish holiday is to connect with local people and become familiar with Spanish communities. This is why talking to locals and befriending Spanish people during your travels across the country is vital. You will learn so much more about the culture and have a more memorable trip if you become accustomed to how Spanish people live. You could try to befriend a Spanish person and spend time in places where locals gather. Traveling to smaller towns and villages can also allow you to connect with local people as there are fewer tourists in those parts of the country. If you want to make local friends you can

- learn some Spanish phrases and greetings.
- spend time at local hotspots.
- ask questions and be more open to talking to Spanish people.
- go to towns and villages where there are no tourists.
- be friendly and greet people or strike up a conversation.
- join in on local traditions and daily activities.
- study the Spanish ways and customs before and during your stay in Spain.

Immerse Yourself in the Spanish Lifestyle

To really become immersed in the Spanish way of life, you need to do as the Spanish do. You should not try to be Spanish, but rather be open to letting go of your prejudices, cultural ways, and views and become more open and excited about really *living* in Spain. This venture would be advisable for a longer stay and for those who are interested in more than being just a tourist. Yes, some people travel abroad so often, but choose to travel as a tourist. This means that they stay in hotels and go to tourist destinations where more tourists spend their time, so they don't really allow themselves to get immersed in the local culture and rather remain living life as a tourist which can seem very similar in most countries. To get a full Spanish experience, you need to leave the tourist nest and be open to really experiencing the lifestyle that is so unique and inherent to the country. Below are some ways you can become more immersed in the Spanish culture:

- Study the culture and observe how locals live.
- Leave your hotel and spend time in the thick of Spanish life.
- Avoid spending most of your days at tourist hotspots and rather spend time where locals live, work, and relax.
- As mentioned, learn some Spanish to understand the culture and connect with locals.
- Walk the streets or take public transport as this is how you can spend time observing and becoming surrounded by Spanish life.
- Shop at grocery stores and markets where the locals shop.
- Attend a church service at one of the local churches to spend time doing routine activities with locals.
- Learn a bit of the history of certain towns and places to understand why and how the locals live and do everyday life.

- Learn about the Spanish traditions and get involved by taking part in annual events or festivals.
- Eat authentic food that locals eat by going to locally-owned restaurants and not tourist eateries that are in hotels or are located in popular restaurant strips.
- Go to museums, libraries, and local parks to learn more about the history and people of Spain.
- Try to not jampack your tourist wishlist with too many sightseeing activities to the point where you have no extra time to spend wandering the streets or sitting down at a local park or eatery to just be and observe the lifestyle.

CHAPTER 4:

EAT, SLEEP, AND RELAX

Taste the Flavors of Spain

Dine Out

Dining out has become a luxury in today's global economic climate. Depending on your budget and your food preferences, Spain has so much to offer when it comes to going out and sitting down for a fresh, well-prepared meal made by a professional chef. Below is a varied list of some restaurants to try out, including the most popular ones with raving reviews:

Madrid

Top five favorites:

- Sobrino de Botín — historic site; *Cuisine*: Spanish; *Address*: Calle de Cuchilleros 17
- Juan of Madrid — Dine with a local Spanish chef
- Cebo — a Michelin star restaurant; *Cuisine*: Spanish-Mediterranean Contemporary; *Address*: Carrera San Jerónimo 34
- Zenith Brunch & Cocktails — *Cuisine*: Café, European; *Address*: Calle Valverde 28
- GastroVía 61 — *Cuisine*: Spanish-Mediterranean; *Address*: Calle de la Flor Baja 3 Hotel Mayorazgo

Restaurants you need to try out:

- El Cocodrilo — *Cuisine*: Spanish, Bar, Vegetarian-Friendly; *Address*: Calle de Pilar de Zaragoza 60
- Ástor — *Cuisine*: International, Mediterranean; *Address*: Calle del Almendro 9
- Los Montes de Galicia — *Cuisine*: Spanish-Mediterranean; *Address*: Calle Azcona 46

- Pilar Akaneya — *Cuisine*: Japanese, Barbecue; *Address*: Calle Espronceda 33

- Andele Ponzano — *Cuisine*: Mexican, Latin; *Address*: Calle Raimundo Fernández Villaverde 26

- Cervecería El Caño — *Cuisine:* Bar, Spanish; *Address*: Calle Cobos de Segovia 30

- Grama Lounge — *Cuisine*: Bar, Venezuelan, Latin; *Address*: Calle de la Cruz 19

- Los Desamparados — *Cuisine*: Spanish, Asian-Fusion, Healthy; *Address*: Costanilla Desamparados 21 Barrio de las letras

- Beytna Restaurante — *Cuisine*: Mediterranean, Middle Eastern; *Address*: Calle Moscatelar 18

- Cedrón Wine Bar — *Cuisine*: Wine Bar, Latin; *Address*: Almendro 25

- Bennu — *Cuisine*: Mediterranean-Latin Fusion, Asian; *Address*: Calle Sandoval 10, 12 Bajo

- Lola Si Mola — *Cuisine*: Spanish-Mediterranean, Healthy; *Address*: Calle de las Huertas 55

Barcelona

Top five favorites:

- Don Kilo Gourmet — *Cuisine*: Italian-Mediterranean; *Address*: Carrer de Còrsega 398

- Vrutal—*Cuisine*: Bar, Healthy and Vegetarian-Friendly; *Address*: Rambla del Poblenou, No. 16 Bajos
- Bodega Biarritz—*Cuisine*: Spanish-Mediterranean; *Address*: Nou de San Francesc 7
- Lato Café—*Cuisine*: American-Latin Fusion; *Address*: Carrer del Bruc 118 Local 1
- Taps—*Cuisine*: Mediterranean-Spanish; *Address*: C/Mare de Deu del Remei, 53

Restaurants you need to try out:

- Blu Bar—*Cuisine*: Bar, Mediterranean and International; *Address*: Rambla de Poblenou, 11 Esquina con Taulat
- La Cava Cakery—*Cuisine*: Dessert, Café; *Address*: Psg. Sant Joan 111
- Wine Mood—*Cuisine*: Bar, Italian, Mediterranean, European; *Address*: Villaroel 26, Barcelona Local 2
- Casa Amàlia 1950—*Cuisine*: Spanish-Mediterranean, Healthy; *Address*: Passatge del Mercat, 14
- Sumac & Mambo—*Cuisine*: Barbecue, Mediterra-nean, Middle Eastern; *Address*: Carrer d'Enric Granados, 30
- Diegos Bar Restaurant—*Cuisine*: Spanish-Mediterranean, International; *Address*: Avinguda

Meridiana 127 Local 1 Entre C//Arago Y C//Valencia

- The Coffee House Barcelona — *Cuisine*: Café, European, Healthy; *Address*: Carrer de València, 143
- Santa Rita Experience — *Cuisine*: Spanish-Mediterranean; *Address*: Carrer de Veneçuela 16
- Toma Ya Street Food — *Cuisine*: Peruvian Street Food, Vegetarian-Friendly; *Address*: Carrer de Nil Fabra 34, 36
- Bar Xapako — *Cuisine*: Bar, Mediterranean; *Address*: Consell de Cent 411

Seville

Top five favorites:

- Vuela Tapas & Cocktail Bar — *Cuisine*: Spanish-Mediterranean; *Address*: Calle de Tomás de Ibarra 20
- Cocome — *Cuisine*: Café, International, Healthy; *Address*: Calle Tarifa 4
- La Sede — *Cuisine*: Spanish-Mediterranean, Healthy; *Address*: Calle Regina Local 7
- La Trastienda De La Sole — *Cuisine*: Spanish; *Address*: Plaza de San Marcos, 1 Local 3
- Heladería Cafetería Francis — *Cuisine*: Café, Healthy, Mediterranean; *Address*: Calle Concejal

Alberto Jimenez Becerril, 8 Prolongación calle Torneo

Restaurants you need to try out:

- Sibuya Urban Sushi Bar Sevilla — *Cuisine*: Japanese, Sushi; *Address*: Calle Albareda 10
- Feria 83 — *Cuisine*: Healthy, Mediterranean; *Address*: Calle de la Feria 83
- Donclaire Azabache — *Cuisine*: Spanish-Mediterranean, Healthy; *Address*: Calle General Polavieja 6 Entre c/Sierpes y Tetuán, junta plaza San Francisco
- La Tizná Honest Grill — *Cuisine*: Steakhouse, Barbecue, Mediterranean; *Address*: Calle de Camila José Cela 1
- Restaurante El Sella Triana — *Cuisine*: Spanish-Mediterranean, Healthy; *Address*: Calle Pureza 4 Triana
- Abaceria del Postigo — *Cuisine*: Spanish-Mediterranean; *Address*: Calle de Tomás de Ilbarra 4
- Bistro Los Tulipanes — *Cuisine*: Dutch-Spanish, International; *Address*: Calle del Almirante Ulloa 8
- El Paseillo — *Cuisine*: Spanish-Mediterranean; *Address*: Calle General Polavieja 4

- Hummo, The Clandestine Grill Company — *Cuisine*: Spanish-Mediterranean, Barbecue; *Address*: Calle Juan de mata Carriazo 4
- Salsitas — *Cuisine*: Fast Food, Spanish-Mediterranean; *Address*: Avenida Pero Mingo 12

Majorca

Top five favorites:

- Sa Cuina De Mercat — *Cuisine*: International and Mediterranean; *Address*: Plaza del Olivar, 5
- Bon VI — *Cuisine*: Seafood, Mediterranean; *Address*: Calle Santa Maria del Cami 3
- Kingfisher Restaurant — *Cuisine*: Seafood, Mediterranean; *Address*: Calle San Ramon de Penyafort 25
- Contrabando Tapas Bar — *Cuisine*: Spanish, Healthy; *Address*: Passeig Jaume III, 2 Local B
- Organic, Restaurante Ecológico — *Cuisine*: Café, Italian-Mediterranean; *Address*: Playa Cala Marsal

Restaurants you need to try out:

- Cannibal Cantina Bistro — *Cuisine*: Spanish-Mediterranean; *Address*: Placa de Sant Antoni 8
- La Vaca Olivia — *Cuisine*: Steakhouse, Latin Barbecue; *Address*: Calle de Margarita Retuerto 3

- Juicy Lucy-Diner & Bar—*Cuisine*: Bar, American; *Address*: Carrer del Torrent, 5
- Petit Café Frozen Yogurt—*Cuisine*: Dessert, Café; *Address*: Passeig Es Traves 23
- Bon Vent Café & Bar—*Cuisine*: Bar, Spanish, Vegetarian-Friendly; *Address*: Av. Bartomeu Riutort, 83
- Izakaya Mallorca—*Cuisine*: Japanese, Sushi; *Address*: Carrer d'Espartero, 15
- Hungry Gastro Food Bar—*Cuisine*: Internation, Mediterranean; *Address*: Carrer d'Enric Alzamora 3
- FaBrick food & more—*Cuisine*: Mediterranean, Contemporary; *Address*: Calle San Magín 84
- Quina Brasa—*Cuisine*: Steakhouse, Mediterranean; *Address*: Placa d'Espanya 5
- Mare Nostrum—*Cuisine*: Spanish-Mediterranean; *Address*: Calle Ric 35

Other Locations

- Meson Asador Casa Rodrigo—*Location*: Tenerife; *Cuisine*: Spanish-Mediterranean; *Address*: Carretera los Menores Taucho, 40
- Dabeke—*Location*: Tenerife; *Cuisine*: Spanish-Mediterranean; *Address*: Calle Candelaria 9
- El Horno De Neptuni—*Location*: Tenerife; *Cuisine*: Spanish-Mediterranean; *Address*: Aveni-

da de Espana 7 CC Terranova Loc 511 Puerto Colon

- Tasca Tierras del Sur — *Location*: Tenerife; *Cuisine*: International, Mediterranean; *Address*: Calle Pedro Gonzalez Gomez 20
- Fish-ART — *Location*: Tenerife; *Cuisine*: Seafood, Italian-Mediterranean; *Address*: Calle Minerva, 16, Costa del Silencio
- La Hormiga — *Location*: Tenerife; *Cuisine*: Spanish-Mediterranean; *Address*: Calle Anchieta 7
- El Taller Seve Díaz — *Location*: Tenerife; *Cuisine*: Spanish-Mediterranean; *Address*: Calle San Felipe 32
- Beer Garden Tenerife — *Location*: Tenerife; *Cuisine*: Bar, British Pub; *Address*: Avenida De Colon Complejo Villaflor B20
- Oliver's Out of Town — *Location*: Tenerife; *Cuisine*: European, Vegetarian-Friendly; *Address*: Carretera General 51, Number 87
- Terraza De Las Flores — *Location*: Málaga; *Cuisine*: Spanish-Mediterranean; *Address*: Plaza De Las Flores, 4
- Anyway WineBar — *Location*: Málaga; *Cuisine*: Spanish-Mediterranean; *Address*: Paseo Reding 15

- La Alacenda de Francis—*Location*: Málaga; *Cuisine*: Spanish, Russian; *Address*: Calle Montalban 1
- Taberna Los 13—*Location*: Málaga; *Cuisine*: Mediterranean; *Address*: Calle Edison, 10
- Mimo Vegan Bistro—*Location*: Málaga; *Cuisine*: International, Contemporary; *Address*: Calle Vendeja 29
- Luxalad Málaga Centro—*Location*: Málaga; *Cuisine*: European, Healthy, Vegetarian-Friendly; *Address*: Calle Fajardo 9
- Alegría Flamenco Gastronomía—*Location*: Málaga; *Cuisine*: Spanish-Mediterranean, Fusion; *Address*: Calle Vélez Málaga 6
- Julia Restaurante—*Location*: Málaga; *Cuisine*: Spanish-Mediterranean; *Address*: Calle San Agustín 11
- Mia Coffee Shop—*Location*: Málaga; *Cuisine*: Café, Healthy, Vegetarian-Friendly; *Address*: Plaza Martires 4
- La Tetería—*Location*: Málaga; *Cuisine*: Dessert, Bar, Café; *Address*: Calle San Agustín 9
- Doña Inés—*Location*: Málaga; *Cuisine*: Spanish-Vegetarian, Vegetarian-Friendly; *Address*: Plaza Poeta Alfonso Canales 5

- Casa Ovi — *Location*: Málaga; *Cuisine*: Spanish-Mediterranea, Fusion; *Address*: Avenida de Sor Teresa Prat 72
- Papá Piquillo — *Location*: Málaga; *Cuisine*: Spanish-Mediterranean, Fusion; *Address*: Calle Cárcer 2
- Restaurante Valle de Mogan — *Location*: Gran Canaria; *Cuisine*: International, Mediterranean; *Address*: Calle Los Pasitos 2
- Ibericos J. Cruz — *Location*: Gran Canaria; *Cuisine*: Spanish, Deli; *Address*: Calle Partera Leonorita 22
- Restaurante El Alpende de Felix — *Location*: Gran Canaria; *Cuisine*: International, Mediterranean; *Address*: La Sorrueda La Fortaleza de Asiste
- Biocreperia Risco Caido — *Location*: Gran Canaria; *Cuisine*: Spanish-Mediterranean; *Address*: Avenida de Matias Vegas 13
- Mol Café — *Location*: Gran Canaria; *Cuisine*: Café, Spanish-Mediterranean; *Address*: Calle de Cadiz 18 Esq Bailen
- Cocó Food & Wines — *Location*: Gran Canaria; *Cuisine*: International, Mediterranean, Contemporary; *Address*: Calle Plácido Domingo, 10
- A Huevo Restaurante — *Location*: Valencia; *Cuisine*: Spanish-Mediterranean; *Address*: Calle de Salamanca 28

- Salad Planet—*Location*: Valencia; *Cuisine*: Healthy, Fast Food; *Address*: Calle Doctor Romangosa 3
- Eggcellent Brunch Café—*Location*: Valencia; *Cuisine*: Café, Healthy, European; *Address*: Avinguda Oest 33
- Infraganti—*Location*: Valencia; *Cuisine*: Italian, Pizza; *Address*: Plaza de la Ciudad Brujas No. 343 AL 347
- d'Sano—*Location*: Granada; *Cuisine*: International, Café; *Address*: Calle San Jerónimo 24
- Palacio Andaluz Almona—*Location*: Granada; *Cuisine*: Moroccan, Mediterranean; *Address*: Calle San Jerónimo, 5
- La Taberna de Kafka—*Location*: Granada; *Cuisine*: Spanish-Mediterranean; *Address*: Calle Huete 2 Barrio del Realejo
- Restaurante Garbo by Melia—*Location*: Granada; *Cuisine*: Spanish, European, Vegetarian-Friendly; *Address*: Calle de Angel Ganivet 7 Melia
- Capitán Amargo Craft Beers—*Location*: Granada; *Cuisine*: Bar, Mediterranean; *Address*: Calle de los Molinos 28
- Tablao Flamenco Jardines de Zoraya—*Location*: Granada; *Cuisine*: Steakhouse, Mediterranean, Contemporary; *Address*: Calle Panaderos 32

- Bella Ciao Pizzeria — *Location*: Granada; *Cuisine*: Italian, Fast Food; *Address*: Calle Muiscoa Vicente Zarzo 3

- Betula Nana — *Location*: Granada; *Cuisine*: Spanish, Healthy, Vegan-Friendly; *Address*: Calle Malaga 9

- The Kitchen 62 — *Location*: Ibiza; *Cuisine*: Mediterranean, Vegetarian-Friendly; *Address*: Carrer Des Calo 62

- Junglebowls — *Location*: Ibiza; *Cuisine*: Japanese-Asian, Sushi; *Address*: Carrer del País Basc 9

- Es Gerret — *Location*: Ibiza; *Cuisine*: Spanish-Mediterranean; *Address*: Calle de Vara de Rey 23 Bajo C

- Can Jesper — *Location*: Ibiza; *Cuisine*: Dutch, International; *Address*: Calle de Pere Escanellas 3

- Street Ibiza — *Location*: Ibiza; *Cuisine*: Bar, Fast Food; *Address*: Carrer del Progré 26

- Restaurante Tic Tac — *Location*: Ibiza; *Cuisine*: Mediterranean, Bar; *Address*: Calle Escalo 23

- Restaurante Cafeteria Pentxo — *Location*: Bilbao; *Cuisine*: Café, European; *Address*: C. Belosticalle 20

- Don Crepe — *Location*: Bilbao; *Cuisine*: International, European; *Address*: Avenida de las Universidades 2

- La Gavilla—*Location*: Bilbao; *Cuisine*: Spanish-Mediterranean, European; *Address*: Colón de Larreategui 32
- Perita—*Location*: Bilbao; *Cuisine*: Seafood, Spanish-Mediterranean; *Address*: Diputacion 1
- Sugarra—*Location*: Bilbao; *Cuisine*: Steakhouse, Spanish-Mediterranean; *Address*: Izaro Mendia-ren Kalea 4

Eat In

If you're feeling lazy or tired from a full day of walking the streets of Spain, there are many wholesome takeout and delivery options for you. Eating in is less pricey than dining out, but it still offers the convenience of not having to go grocery shopping and cooking. Ordering takeout can also be a more budget-friendly option for when your accommodation does not allow for cooking while your pocket also does not allow for eating out every night. Ordering in is a perfect balance of time and money-saving. Below is a list of some establishments that offer authentic Spanish and international cuisine that can be enjoyed in the comfort of your temporary home in Spain:

- Restaurante Yunie Kebab—*Location*: Madrid; *Cuisine*: Lebanese; *Address*: C. de Meléndez Valdés 63

- Tino—*Location*: Barcelona; *Cuisine*: Italian, Fast Food; *Address*: Carrer de Muntaner 102

- Kimchi Mama—*Location*: Barcelona; *Cuisine*: Korean-Asian; *Address*: Callao 12

- El Aliño—*Location*: Madrid; *Cuisine*: Home-cooked Fusion Food; *Address*: Calle Espíritu Santo 2

- Cacho & Pepe—*Location*: Granada; *Cuisine*: Home-cooked Italian Food; *Address*: Calle Colcha 6

- Pupu Poke—*Location*: Granada; *Cuisine*: Hawaiian; *Address*: Calle San Isidro 15

- Tap Tim — *Location*: Granada; *Cuisine*: Asian-Fusion; *Address*: Avenida de las Palmeras 75, Nevada Shopping Center
- Estambul — *Location*: Granada; *Cuisine*: Turkish Shawarma; *Address*: C. Crucero Baleares 6
- TGB: The Good Burger — *Location*: Nationwide; *Cuisine*: Burgers, Fast Food
- Sanissimo — *Location*: Madrid; *Cuisine*: Healthy, Vegan; *Address*: Calle San Vicente Ferrer 28
- Oink — *Location*: Madrid; *Cuisine*: Spanish Sandwiches; *Address*: Calle Gran Via 22
- Food Truck — *Location*: Madrid; *Cuisine*: American Fast Food; *Address*: Calle San Lucas 11
- Museo del Jamón — *Location*: Madrid; *Cuisine*: Deli, Spanish; *Address*: Calle Mayor 7
- Takos al Pastor — *Location*: Madrid; *Cuisine*: Mexican; *Address*: Calle de la Abada 2
- Goiko Grill — *Location*: Madrid; *Cuisine*: American, Cafeteria; *Address*: Calle de María de Molina 20
- La Campana — *Location*: Madrid; *Cuisine*: Spanish Sandwiches, Tapas; *Address*: Calle de las Botoneras 6
- Munchies Hot Dog — *Location*: Madrid; *Cuisine*: Hot Dogs, Fast Food; *Address*: Calle de las Huertas 25

Shop the Local Markets

While eating out and trying new restaurants and bars is always a great way to really feel like you are on holiday, it's also smart to shop like a local, or at least explore local markets. Spain, like many European countries, has an array of markets that are made up of fresh fruit and vegetables, street food, seafood, and local arts and crafts. When you want to experience the beating heart of a Spanish city or town, visit one of these local markets to immerse yourself in the energy of Spanish culture, cuisine, and creativity:

Madrid

- Mercado San Miguel. Authentic Spanish market; *Location*: Plaza de San Miguel; *Opening Hours*: Sunday-Thursday from 10 a.m. to 12 a.m., Friday and Saturday from 10 a.m. to 1 a.m.
- El Rastro. Flea market; *Location*: Calle de la Ribera de Curtidores; *Opening Hours*: Sunday from 9 a.m. to 3 p.m.
- Mercado de Navidada de Plaza. Christmas Market; *Location*: Plaza Mayor; *Opening Hours*: November 24th through December 31st from 10 a.m. to 10:30 p.m.
- Mercado de San Antón. Neighborhood market; *Location*: C. de Figueroa 24, Chueca; *Opening*

Hours: Monday-Sunday from 9:30 a.m. to 12 a.m.

- Mercado de Maravilla. Neighborhood market; *Location*: C. de Bravo Murilla, 122, Tetuán; *Opening Hours*: Monday-Friday from 9 a.m. to 2 p.m. and 5 p.m. to 8 p.m., Saturday from 9 a.m. to 3 p.m.

Barcelona

- Mercado de La Boqueria. Spanish Food market; *Location*: Rambla, 91; *Opening Hours*: Monday-Saturday from 8 a.m. to 8:30 p.m.
- Fira de Santa Llúcia. Christmas market; *Location*: Avinguda de la Catedral; *Opening Hours*: November 24th through December 23rd from 10 a.m. to 10:30 p.m.
- Mercado del Centro de Vilanova i la Geltrú. Local Spanish food market; *Location*: Plaça Soler i Carbonell; *Opening Hours*: Monday-Friday from 8 a.m. to 2 p.m., with additional hours on Tuesday and Friday from 5 p.m. to 8 p.m., Saturday from 7 a.m. to 2:30 p.m.

Others

- Mercado Central. Spanish food market; *Location*: Plaza Ciudad de Brujas, Valencia; *Opening Hours*: Monday-Saturday from 7 a.m. to 3 p.m.

- Alcaicería Markert. Crafts market; *Location*: Calle Alcaiceria 1, Granada; *Opening Hours*: Monday-Saturday from 11 a.m. to 8 p.m.

- Mercado de Abastos. Food market; *Location*: Rúa das Ameas, Santiago de Compostela, A Coruña; *Opening Hours*: Monday-Saturday from 8 a.m. to 3 p.m.

- Mercado de la Ribera. Food market; *Location*: Erribera Kalea, Bilbao; *Opening Hours*: Monday-Friday 8 a.m. to 2:30 p.m. and 5 p.m. to 8 p.m., Saturday from 8 a.m. to 3 p.m.

- Mercado Central. Food market; *Location*: Avenida Alfonso X El Sabio, 10, Alicante; *Opening Hours*: Monday-Friday from 7 a.m. to 2:30 p.m., Saturday from 7 a.m. to 3 p.m.

- Mercado Central de Atarazanas. Food market; *Location*: Calle Atarazanas, 10, Málaga; *Opening Hours*: Monday-Saturday from 8 a.m. to 2 p.m.

- Mercado Central. Food market; *Location*: Plaza de la Libertad, Cádiz; *Opening Hours*: Monday-Friday from 9 a.m. to 4 p.m., 7 p.m. to 12 a.m., Saturday from 9 a.m. to 4 p.m., 8 p.m. to 1 a.m.

- Mercado Colon. Local market; *Location*: Carrer de Jorge Juan, 19, València; *Opening Hours*: Sunday-Thursday from 8 a.m. to 1 a.m., Friday and Saturday from 8 a.m. to 2 a.m.

- Mercado de la Magdalena. Food market; *Location*: 15402, Ferrol; *Opening Hours*: Monday-Thursday 5 a.m. to 4 p.m., Friday 5 a.m. to 4 p.m. and 6 p.m. to 9 p.m., Saturday from 5 a.m. to 4 p.m.
- Mercado de Nuestra Señora de África. Food market; *Location*: Avenida de San Sebastián, 51, Santa Cruz de, Tenerife; *Opening Hours*: Monday-Saturday from 6 a.m. to 2 p.m., Sunday from 7 a.m. to 2 p.m.
- A Batea do Mercado. Food market; *Location*: Rúa Serra, 5, Pontevedra; *Opening Hours*: Tuesday-Thursday from 1:30 p.m. to 3:30 p.m., Friday and Saturday from 1:30 p.m. to 3:30 p.m., 8:30 p.m. to 11:30 p.m.

Accommodation for All

When traveling abroad, accommodation can always be a tricky factor in your planning and even your actual stay in a foreign country. A great tip to finding the perfect accomodation for you is to know what your interests and expectations are for your trip. Follow your travel wishlist, and find places that will accommodate your travel needs. For instance, if you are more of a beach hopper, staying at a hotel or guest house that is located along the beach or even near the beach would be a wise move. Before you pick your accommodation for your travels in and around Spain, know what makes you excited about your trip and also know what attractions you would like to experience.

We have compiled lists of accommodations across the country from budget-friendly stays to local homestays and even luxury hotels. We have it all. These lists will also give you an idea of the pricing of accommodation in the different regions of Spain and equip you for your holiday.

Budget Living

Hostels, cheaper hotels and motels, and private rooms are the most budget-friendly types of accommodations. Below is a list of budget-friendly accommodations across the country of Spain:

- Hotel-Apartamentos Peña Santa. *Location*: La plaza s/n, Onís; *Price*: €54–100
- Casual de las Olas San Sebastián. *Location*: Pio XII. arena Plaza 3, Amara, San Sebastián; *Price*: €60–260
- Hostal Ballesta. *Location*: Calle Ballesta 5, Madrid; *Price*: € 50–100 per night
- Hostal la Perla Asturiana. *Location*: Plaza Santa Cruz 3, Madrid; *Price*: €40–55 per night
- Hostal Zamora. *Location*: Plaza Vazquez de Mella 4, 1 Izda, Madrid; *Price*: €45 per night
- Hostal Palacio Luna. *Location*: Calle de la Luna, 6, 3D, Centro, Madrid; *Price*: €60–110 per night

- House in Zarza. *Location*: Zarza, Murcia; *Price*: from €66 per night
- Holiday house in Almuñécar. *Location*: Almuñécar, Andalusia; *Price*: from €44 per night
- Apartment in Santa Cruz. *Location*: Santa Cruz de Tenerife, Canary Islands; *Price*: from €58 per night
- Casa Don Pedro in Peguera. *Location*: Peguera, Majorca Island; *Price*: from €35 per night
- Apartment on North Beach. *Location*: Peñíscola, Valencia; *Price*: from €22 per night
- Apartment in Rural Gallego. *Location*: Ourense, Galicia; *Price*: from €32 per night.
- Good Stay Madrid. *Location*: Embajadores, 14, City Center, Madrid; *Price*: €50–80 per night
- 8 Calle Tangara La Gloria. *Location*: Santa Cruz de Tenerife; *Price*: €41 per night
- EDI Astoria. *Location*: Emilio Calzadilla 11 Esquina San Juan Bautista, Santa Cruz de Tenerife; *Price*: from €58–68 per night.

Luxury Living

For someone who has money to spend and wants to have a luxurious time in the Mediterranean, living in luxury suites is perfect. With room service, air conditioning, central locations, and all the amenities you can think of, living in a hotel with international standards can make your stay in Spain even more carefree. The list compiled below gives you an idea of the cost and variety of hotel and luxury stays in Spain:

- Masia Can Canyes & Spa. *Location*: Cami de Can Canyes s/n Masia Alt Penedès, San Lorenzo de Hortóns; *Price*: €80–150 per night
- Izaila Plaza Catalunya. *Location*: Ronda de Sant Pere 7, Planta Principal, Eixample, Barcelona; *Price*: €94–180 per night
- Casa del Mediterraneo. *Location*: Carrer Valencia, 226, Eixample, Barcelona. *Price*: from €130 per night
- Uma House Pau Claris. *Location*: Carrer de Pau Claris, 72, Eixample, Barcelona; *Price*: €80–130 per night
- Violeta Boutique. *Location*: Caspe, 38, Eixample, Barcelona; *Price*: €117–126 per night
- Casa Boutique La Pila del Plato. *Location*: Alhondiga, 58, Old Town, Seville; *Price*: €50–150 per night.
- Casa de Mariana. *Location*: Calle Mariana de Pineda, 10, Old Town, Seville; *Price*: €90–120 per night.

- Suites del Arenal. *Location*: Calle Antón de la Cerda 8, Old Town, Seville; *Price*: €80–120 per night
- Casa Catalina. *Location*: Carrer de Pou, 35, Santa Catalina, Palma de Mallorca; *Price*: €60–115 per night
- The Principal Madrid Hotel. *Location*: C/ Marques de Valdeiglesias, 1, City Center, Madrid; *Price*: €280–367 per night
- Grand Hotel Central. *Location*: Via Laietana, 30, Gothic, Barcelona; *Price*: from €200–250 per night.
- Sud Ibiza Suites. *Location*: Calle Ramón Muntaner 34, Ibiza Town; *Price*: from €100–400 per night
- Apartaments B-Llobet Sun & Confort. *Location*: Avenida Pere Matutes Noguera, 20, Ibiza Town; *Price*: from €130–240 per night

Local Living

Some travelers want to feel like locals and be fully immersed in the culture. Staying in a local Spanish home is an easy, smart, and often more cost-effective way to become part of the community you are staying in. While some areas may be less tourist-friendly, they allow you to feel like you are truly part of Spanish life as you are literally living like a local by staying in locally-owned homes. The list below reveals the diversity of Spanish local living, from budget-friendly homestays in the suburbs to grand and exclusive estates:

- Hotel 3 Alpacas. *Location*: Barrio Cdamancio 20, San Justo, La Campa; *Price*: €70–80 per night
- Casas Rurales Los Algarrobales. *Location*: Carril de las Minas, s/n, El Gastor; *Price*: €125–139 per night
- Las Musas Hotel. *Location*: C/ Real Somera 41, La Cuenca; *Price*: €84–92 per night
- Hotel Mirador de Barcia. *Location*: Barcia, 3, Ribeira de Piquin; *Price*: €77–85 per night
- Hotel Can Riera. *Location*: Calle Passeig de Sa Creu 4 y 7, Moscari; *Price*: €88–116 per night
- Villa Camamila. *Location*: Cielo de Bonaire, Balearic Islands; *Price*: from €216 per night
- Villa 'Mi Amor.' *Location*: Alfamar, Salobreña, Andalucía. Price: from €82 per night
- House in Fornalutx. *Location*: Fornalutx, West Majorca, Balearic Islands; *Price*: €120 per night
- Apartment in Madrid. *Location*: Vallecas, Madrid; *Price*: from €76 per night
- Apartment in Madrid. *Location*: Cortes, Madrid. *Price*: from €72 per night

- Resort in Elorrio. *Location*: Elorrio, Basque Country; *Price*: from €180 per night
- La Quintana de la Foncalada, self-catering farmstay. *Location*: Rural Cantabric Rocky Coast, Asturias; *Price*: from €60 per night
- Villa Vista Mar. *Location*: Tijarafe, Canary Islands; *Price*: from €160 per night
- House Gregal 81. *Location*: El Mas Pinell, Catalonia; *Price*: from €70 per night
- Luxury Apartment in Los Gigantes. *Location*: Acantilados de los Gigantes, West Tenerife, Canary Islands; *Price*: from €105 per night
- Los Lilos gîta. *Location*: Siguenza, Castilla, La Mancha; *Price*: from €67 per night
- House Enriqueta. *Location*: Playa de Muro, Alcudia, Balearic Islands; *Price*: from €98 per night
- Can Benet Pisa. *Location*: Calella de Palafrugell, Catalonia; *Price*: from €42 per night
- Beachhouse Sa Barca. *Location*: Cala Santanyí, Balearic Islands; *Price*: from €195 per night.
- Villa in Cala en Porter. *Location*: Cala en Porter, Menorca; *Price*: from €84 per night
- Villa Dajabe Sayalonga. *Location*: Carraspite, Andalusia; *Price*: from €215 per night.

- Apartment near Canyelles Cove. *Location*: Lloret de Mar, Catalonia; *Price*: from €28 per night
- Apartment Blasco Ibañez 3. *Location*: Canet d'en Berenguer, Valencia; *Price*: from €106 per night
- Chalet in Pollença. *Location*: Pollença, Balearic Islands; *Price*: from €163 per night
- Ventanas al Mediterráneo. *Location*: Torrox, Andalusia; *Price*: from €183 per night
- Cortijo Los Alazores. *Location*: Huétor-Tájar, Andalusia; *Price*: from €93 per night.

Unique Experiences to Unwind or Refresh

- La Tomatina—the annual tomato food fight festival held in the town of Bunol is a fun tradition of throwing juicy tomatoes at one another.
- Sierra Nevada National Park—a stunning nature reserve with amazing views from hiking trails.
- The Rioja Wine Harvest Festival—an annual festival celebrating local wines.
- El Caminito del Rey—a trail through the gorge of El Chorro.
- Camino de Santiago—a well-known pilgrimage that takes up to 30 days to complete.

- A night at El Eshavira—a hidden gem of a bar in Granada that offers a great flamenco show and live music.
- Ruta del Flysch—a national reserve offers trails and picnic spots with incredible views.
- The Doñana National Park—a reserved area for camping, hiking, and many outdoor activities.
- San Fermín Festival—the annual running of the bulls festival.

CHAPTER 5:

UPDATED COVID-19 TRAVEL PROTOCOLS

Traveling During Covid-19

We know that the Covid-19 virus, because it is a serious contagion, has made it almost impossible to enjoy a care-free holiday in the last two years. We've had to receive many stories, global messages, and policy changes in the years 2020 and 2021. It seems as if we have been in a waiting room, especially for those of us who are avid travelers and wanderlust. Traveling is precious; spending time with other people and connecting with a community are activities we used to take for granted no longer will in 2022.

This year has given us some clarity as we have persevered and survived the two devastating years of the Covid-19 pandemic. Now is the time to make wise decisions and take opportunities to travel when and where we can. If you are planning to travel to Spain, or any country for that matter, in the year 2022, you will need to acknowledge the fact that there is still an ongoing pandemic. The world is not what it used to be, but it is slowly getting better and brighter. There are more freedoms than we had a year ago. We have adapted to our current global situation, and we have been able to find ways, even with some compromise, to still have fun and be safe at the same time. If you are ready to go back to exploring different cities and cultures, then knowing how to travel in a pandemic needs to be a priority. Spain has followed many global Covid-19 protocols throughout the two years of the pandemic, but there have been many updates made from the beginning of 2020 to now in 2022. We know that everyone has had to adjust how they go about everyday life and traveling has been affected on a large scale. While many have their own opinions and ways of combating or living through Covid-19, whether it be views regarding current policies or certain medical conditions, this chapter provides the official guidelines from Spanish authorities. We will look at the common protocols for public spaces, what is expected from you when you arrive and travel in Spain, as well as the country's current approach to overseas travelers.

Covid-19 Protocols and Habits

- Be wise and ensure you have health insurance for travel to cover any medical emergencies.
- Remain responsible when around other people by following local laws about protecting yourself and others from Covid-19.
- Follow social distancing of 1.5 meters.
- Carry a face mask with you and wear it in enclosed public places and outdoor areas where there are groups of people and gatherings like shopping malls, markets, and public events.
- Follow the specific protocols of establishments that are set out like in restaurants, hotels, shops, etc.
- Wash your hands frequently with soap and water, and sanitize when you are moving in and out of public spaces where no water is available.
- Carry a "Covid passport" — a vaccination card to prove that you are vaccinated if needed for entrance into social places like restaurants, bars, hospitals, etc.
- Follow the overnight curfew of some regions.
- Ensure you do not attend or host gatherings that exceed the specified maximum number of people in certain venues.

- Be aware of capacity restrictions at certain private and public spaces.
- Quarantine if you tested positive for Covid-19 or show any symptoms, and notify others with whom you have been in contact.

Updated Spanish Covid-19 Policies and Travel

While healthy measures concerning the spread of Covid-19 can vary across areas and spaces, there are national policies and current Covid-19 laws that have been updated. Due to the ever-changing nature of the virus, with the new, more contagious strains emerging like Omicron, Spain has its own list of "risk" and "high risk" countries. The list of "high risk" countries is updated often and is always changing, but individuals who are from countries on this list cannot enter Spain without a recent negative Covid test. The list of nations that are deemed "risk" countries that require travelers from these countries to enter Spain either fully vaccinated or with a recent negative Covid test include non-EU and non-Schengen countries. Countries outside of the EU that have been exempt from this "risk" include Chile, Hong Kong, Indonesia, New Zealand, Rwanda, Saudi Arabia, South Korea, Taiwan.

Knowing your country's status can help you make any last-minute adjustments to your travel plans. You need to keep an open mind and be realistic when it comes to the changes in Spanish and European travel policies. There have been and will be changes made throughout the year of 2022; therefore, keeping up to date and following Spanish health department broadcasts are essential when planning your trip. Right now, the country requires people to follow regional rules, which means policies vary from province to province and even among institutions. While there is the universal Covid 'etiquette' adopted by most, which has been advised by the World Health Organization (WHO), you still need to remain vigilant when traveling across the country. Spanish authorities and certain private institutions have the right to ask for our identification (ID or Passport) and proof of vaccination, as well as the right to ban individuals from institutions for not wearing masks in places outside their place of residence. While masks were mandatory for indoor gatherings, Spain has enforced stricter rules about mask wearing to the point where face masks can be expected to be worn in outdoor spaces.

Spain's travel policy at the moment allows any individual from any country to travel in and out of the country with the correct travel documents as per usual with the addition of Covid-19 factors. These additional policies include vaccinations and testing, with the exception of those from European and Schengen countries.

CHAPTER 6:

THE CITIES AND
ISLANDS OF SPAIN

Explore the Main Cities

Cities, Towns, Suburbs, and Villages

Madrid

The biggest city in Spain and its capital, Madrid is a hub of culture and opportunity. Due to its rich history and high population, Madrid is central to Spanish life and your trip to Spain. The climate is cold and windy in the winter months and hot and dry in the summer months. The consistent and comfortable weather, the many amenities, and the merging of cultures from expats, tourists, and locals make it impossible not to enjoy this city. There is so much to do and see, including the many museums, bars, plazas, and restaurants. This city has so much to offer!

70

Barcelona

As the second-largest and most popular destination of travel for tourists, Barcelona is a top holiday city. Despite the high population and so many attractions, there is a laid-back feel about the city. Barcelona not only provides city life like bustling markets, nightlife, and high-class restaurants, but it is also a city of art and distinctive Spanish architecture. The many buildings designed by iconic architect Antoni Gaudí and other modernist artists are on display across the city. It also offers hidden streets and historical places (like the Gothic Quarter Barcelona) that showcase the vibrancy of Spanish life and culture with the many colors, textures, smells, and sounds of the humming city.

Valencia

As the third biggest city in the country, Valencia offers many tourist and local attractions. The city is a popular sport for many European cruises due to its sunny and warm weather for over 300 days of the year. Locals and tourists enjoy the natural beauty and history the city has to offer. The treasures of the city can be seen in its display of Roman architecture and Muslim influence that has manifested in Valencia's local customs, culture, language, and unique way of life.

Seville

This is the capital city of the Andalusia region of Spain. Located in southern Spain along the Guadalquivir

River, the city offers warm and sunny weather — a perfect Mediterranean climate. Not only does Seville provide pleasant weather, it also offers an array of attractions. This ancient city has landmarks that hold a blend of cultural history. Some attractions include the Alcazar Castle with Moorish roots as well as the Gothic Seville Cathedral that is home to the tomb of Christopher Columbus. Along with historic features, the city also offers a contemporary and youthful lifestyle with its popular tapas bars, exhibitions, and theaters.

Zaragoza

This northeastern city, located on the Ebro River, showcases its history through its many Roman and Gothic buildings. Being the capital of the Aragon region, Zaragoza has to offer historical churches, contemporary establishments, and many natural attractions that make it one of the top cities in Spain.

Malaga

With scenic beaches and an authentic Mediterranean flair, this city is a tourist favorite. Located in the south of Spain, on the Costa del Sol, there has been an influx of tourists and an increase in tourist-friendly businesses like hotels, restaurants, and bars. The position of Malaga — between mountains and ocean —

as well as the climate being hot in summer and mild in winter make it an obvious choice for a beachside vacation. There is still history in this city with the 8th-century Moorish fortress, Alcazaba, being a tourist attraction to this day. For a beach lover who enjoys a relaxed summer trip, this city is the place to be.

Murcia

This city is smaller than the other cities in Spain. Founded around 825, this city has a lot to offer. The history of the city is one of creativity. Murcia was the center of materials like ceramics, silks, and paper manufacturing. The city is also known for its agricultural industry, specifically fresh fruit, vegetables, and flowers, which can be seen throughout its countryside. Its industry flourished due to its geography and fertile land, being surrounded by the Segura River, which makes it a beautiful place to admire and appreciate its local produce and scenery.

Bilbao

This city is a popular place to admire the art of Spain. For instance, Bilbao is the home of the Guggenheim art museum in Spain. The traditional and contemporary Spanish cultures merge in this city, where there are modern attractions as well as local food markets and tapas bars situated close to museums and buildings that are hundreds of years old. The city is a place of synergy as there can be a contemporary, Michelin-star restaurant near a smaller, local restaurant where you can experience local cuisine. Like many cities in Spain, Bilbao is a hub of culture and art where today's wonders are integrated with the wonders of the past.

Granada

This city is located in the south of the Andalusia region on the foot of the Sierra Nevada mountains. This is a culturally-rich city and showcases true Spanish culture. The city holds the famous medieval Alhambra with Moorish architecture. Granada also offers lively, more contemporary attractions like tapas bars and restaurants, flamenco clubs, and cafés. These new establishments have also increased due to the largest student population in the country being in Granada.

Cadaques

This Catalonian town is situated by the water, along the bay of Punta de Sa Costa. Not only can you enjoy what a seaside town has to offer, but you can also explore the nature reserve of this town with hiking trails and breathtaking views. The village itself is a picturesque and quaint Spanish-style landscape, with its traditional Spanish-style homes that still stand today against a background of blue and green.

Albarracín

This medieval village is located 4,000 feet above sea level. The village seems like it was preserved. There is a castle and cathedral as well as the main square that can be explored. In September, the village hosts the annual Santa Maria Festival which creates a lively, buzzing atmosphere. Throughout the year, the village is a quiet sanctuary formed by its historic walls. The cobblestone streets and alleyways of this village will make you feel like you have traveled back in time as you admire all its unique charm. Outside the village, you can go on hiking trails to soak in the quiet of the hills of Albarracín.

Alcalá del Júcar

This small town overlooks the Júcar river. While appearing minute when compared to other Spanish towns, Alcalá del Júcar has so much to offer. The attractions include Plaza de Toros and cave houses which make this town so special, standing out among other smaller towns. Due to its geography and architecture, the town offers a once in a lifetime experience — dining in a cave!

Sóller

Despite being in Majorca, this island town provides a more authentic Spanish experience as it is away from the tourist hubs of the city of Majorca. Offering a more traditional stay, one can enjoy the peace that its mountains and waters offer. This town, with its port, provides all that small Spanish coastal towns have and more. There are also great sights to try out like the exhibition of Picasso's ceramics at Salla Picasso and Salla Miro. The town also offers great seafood, bars, restaurants, cafés, a vibrant town square, and an old church.

Potes, Cantabria

Unlike the other villages of Spain, Potes is covered in moss and all the greenery of its mountainous countryside. It also has the Deva river running through the center of it, which makes this village even more unique. The village is iconic for its stone arches and other natural landmarks like the limestone peak of Naranjo de Bulnes. In addition to historic architecture and surrounding natural beauty, the village of Potes offers delicious local cuisine, Cantabrian dishes like chickpea pies, and traditional stews that are made and enjoyed by locals.

Combarro, Galicia

This tiny fishing village, located in the region of Rias Baixas, is for those who want to escape the tourists and the busyness of the cities and rather experience true Spanish laid-back living. While it is still a coastal town, it offers historical huts and an idyllic harbor where you can take in the sea. The seafood, of course, is a bonus as you can get fresh shellfish and local dishes like *pulpo gallego* (Galician spiced octopus) at prices far from the tourist prices of restaurants in other oceanside cities.

Hondarribia, Basque Country

This iconic village is located between the Spanish and French border. The colorful architecture of this village makes for a picturesque experience when admiring the many local houses in the village center. Hondarribia is a coastal village, which means you can enjoy the shores of the local beach. In addition to its history and sandy beaches, the village is also conveniently situated near wine regions for those who enjoy their wine. The vineyards in this area produce authentic Spanish wines, such as Txakoli which is a dry and lightly sparkling white wine. Despite the isolated location, far from the central places of Spain, this seaside village has unique local offerings for its inhabitants and tourists alike.

Mogarraz, Castile and Léon

This tiny medieval town is isolated due to its geography; it is situated between mountain ranges and national parks. Its isolation has made it a town stuck in the medieval era, and that is not something to complain about. With only about 300 inhabitants, Mogarraz has been able to preserve its history in its architecture and its expression of the many centuries that have shaped it. The town showcases its contrasting influences like Arabic style to Jewish culture. The houses that still stand reveal this town's age, with timber bars and stone with carved out symbols. The artistry of Mogarraz can be seen throughout Spain, as the town is the birthplace of distinct jewelry work and embroidery.

Island Adventures

Islands, Natural Beauties, and Outdoor Activities

Balearic Islands

- Palma, or Palma de Majorca, is one of the main cities among the islands of Spain and is the capital city of the island of Majorca. The city is located in Palma Bay and attracts tourists for many months of the year. The popularity of the city, and the island of Majorca, is due to its location in the warm and inviting Mediterranean Sea, as well as its pleasant climate. The city is tourist-friendly with all the amenities and establishments needed like hotels, hostels, homestays, as well as beach bars and restaurants. The history of Palma can also be observed by visiting the Royal Palace of la Almudena as well as the local cathedral. The island's natural beauty also makes it favorable for those more adventurous travelers who enjoy the ocean and everything Spain's landscapes have to offer. The island of Majorca is known for its beaches like Cala Llombards, Cala Torta, Canyamel, and Es Trenc.

- Menorca is a more idyllic island with fewer tourists than its counterparts, protecting the wildlife and pristine beaches. The island offers beautiful beaches along its coastline like Caló Blanc, Son Saura, Pregonda, as well as the Camí de Cavalls, a 700-year-old path that is perfect for birdwatching and wildlife exploration as well as coves that are safe to swim in.

- Ibiza, known as the party capital, is an island that attracts many tourists from all over the world. It is full of energy and vibrant nightlife. It also offers natural attractions, such as beaches like Cala d'Hort, Cala Conta, Cala Codolar, and Aguas Blancas.

- The isle of Formentera offers beaches with boardwalks along the shore of soft white sand.

Beaches include Illetas beach, Levante, Migjorn, and the family-friendly Cala Saona.

Top sights and activities:

- Paddle and snorkel in Majorca's waters.
- Explore the underground lakes of the Cuevas del Drach.
- Roam the port town of Mahón's markets and charming streets.
- Enjoy the nightlife of Ibiza's popular bars and nightclubs.
- Explore the old town of Ciutadella's medieval streets and Gothic architecture.
- Do water sports like jet skiing, scuba diving, pedal boating, and water-skiing at the "Blue Flag" beach, Playa de Muro.
- Walk along the vibrant promenade of Puerto Pollensa.
- See the Bellver Castle and the Cathedral of Santa Maria in Palma.
- Shop at the traditional Inca market in Majorca.
- Do the Torrent de Pareis hike through the Tramuntana mountains.
- Spend the day at Aqualand El Arenal water park in Palma.
- Go on a safari drive through Menorca's breath-taking landscapes.

- Visit the zoo in Majorca.
- Go on a wine tour and learn about the wine-making process of regional wines in Majorca.
- Go birdwatching at Es Grau beach.
- Go horse riding along the green hilly landscape in Majorca.
- Play mini-golf at Golf Fantasia in Palma Nova.

Canary Islands

- Tenerife. One of the more popular islands of the country, Tenerife is well-known for its pristine beaches and natural beauty. While there are tourist hotspots, this island offers a range of outdoor and indoor activities due to many unspoilt landscapes and historical buildings. The port of Santa Cruz has grown in popularity and is a tourist destination in the peak seasons while the region operates as an oil-processing and agricultural hub to provide for the country of Spain.

- Gran Canaria. This is another popular tourist destination among the many islands of Spain with—like the rest of them—warm and sunny summer months and crystal clear waters. This island has grown its tourism industry in recent decades due to its location, natural beauty, tourist-friendly infrastructure, and diverse history seen in its architecture.
- Fuerteventura. This island offers beautiful beaches with deep blue waters contrasted with the light sand on its shore. The rolling sand dunes also make this island stand out from the rest.
- La Palma. This island is known for its stunning views, beaches, and opportunities for water adventures like snorkeling, swimming, boating, and exploring its waterfalls. Due to its great beaches and infrastructure, the island is often enjoyed by tourists and locals alike.
- Lanzarote. This island is a destination that offers unique natural beauty. It has beaches, mountainous landscapes, and even lava fields. The history, seen in the art and architecture, of this island also makes it a must-see place for those who want a more scenic and relaxed holiday. Due to its climate, there is also a growing wine industry on the island.

- La Gomera. With a unique coastline and mountainous landscapes, this island is a true treasure. While the island used to be isolated, relying on its natural resources, it has grown its tourism industry in recent years. There is an airport and a few tourist attractions that showcase the rich history of the island.
- El Hierro. One of the smaller islands of Spain, it offers mountainous landscapes and many unspoilt spots to admire the views it provides you. This island does not have as many tourist-friendly sights or infrastructure compared to the other Canary Islands, but it does provide locals with agricultural products and tourists the opportunity to escape the booming tourism industry and busyness experienced on the other islands.

Top sights and activities:

- Hike along the peaks of Gran Canaria.
- Admire the waterfalls of La Palma.
- Walk through the unspoilt fields and trails in El Hierro.
- Snorkel in the waters of the Canary Islands to discover unique fish and a shipwreck.
- Go surf the waves of the beaches.
- Enjoy water adventures like boat rides, kayaking, and paddle boardings.
- Explore the many historical churches and architecture across the archipelago.
- Soak up the sun on the many unspoilt or popular beaches.

- Go on retreats or lessons that help you relax like yoga, meditation, massages, and local therapies such as thalassotherapy.
- Go wine-tasting in regions of Lanzarote, La Palma, or Tenerife.
- Admire the wildlife at Laro Park.
- Go whale-watching in the southwest of Gran Canaria.
- Adventure through the Timanfaya National Park.
- Visit the historic town of La Laguna.
- Take a once in a lifetime trip to see the mysterious Pirámides de Güímar.

Walk the Streets of Spain

Tourist-Friendly Streets

- Gran Vía
- Paseo de la Castellana
- Calle de Preciados
- Puerta del Sol

- Paseo del Prado
- Calle Huertas
- Calle Mayor
- Calle de Segovia
- Passeig del Born
- Calle de Mateos Gago
- Calle Sant Miquel
- Seven Streets

Winding and Hidden Streets

- Calle Cava Baja
- Calle del Espíritu Santo
- Carrer de Joaquín Cosat
- Carrer dels Flassaders
- Carrer d'Evarist Arnús
- Passatge de la Concepció
- Plaça de Sant Felip Neri
- Plaza Escuelas de Cristo
- Calle Verde
- Ghost station of Chamberí
- Columns of the temple of Augustus, in the Gothic Quarter, Paradís street 10
- Plaza de San Felipe Neri
- Valldigna Gate
- The Garden of the Hesperides

CONCLUSION

We have guided you through the different stages of planning and going on a trip to Spain. No matter what your holiday dreams are or your choice of food, drink, activity, this guide has given you the information and tricks needed to enjoy the holiday you have always envisioned. Every traveler is different just like every person is unique. This is why our guide has offered you a range of methods and activities you can try out when in Spain. We went through it all and now we have come to the end of our journey, while your journey is only just beginning!

In Chapter 1, we discussed all the details and steps involved in planning an international trip. Time management was key in this discussion in addition to budgeting. Remember, each person has their own budget and a specific length of stay, so it is important to form a travel plan around your personal needs and travel desires. No matter how long your stay is, it is only natural to try to get as much out of your holiday as possible. The balance between staying busy and relaxing on holiday is a skill. There is no need for burnout when you are on holiday. Instead, we want to ensure that you are able to plan out a trip that works for you and not against you in terms of time and budget. No one wants to come home from a trip to Spain with zero energy and no cash left over. Knowing what you want out of your trip and doing your research beforehand will allow you to plan a trip that will offer you the most out of your stay.

Following on from planning tips and tricks, Chapter 2 focused on the many attractions Spain has to offer. Once you have planned out the timeline of your Spanish holiday, you can then create your holiday wishlist, consisting of all the popular must-see and more hidden sights of Spain. From popular museums to more quaint hidden treasures, this chapter gave you a variety of places and spaces to explore in Spain.

When exploring the cities and villages of Spain, you need to always remember where you are and the local culture of the place. This is why in Chapter 3 we discussed some ways you can become immersed in the vibrant Spanish culture. From learning Spanish phrases to spending time with locals and taking part in local traditions, we covered the many opportunities you have to really become part of this beautiful and lively country.

In Chapter 4, we took the next step by looking at what Spain has to offer you. Eating and sleeping, in addition to relaxing and adventuring, is so important when on holiday. Therefore, this chapter involved lists of where to eat out and eat in, where to stay, and where to explore so you can experience unique Spanish activities. Again, we looked at a variety of restaurants and bars, hotels and hostels, and even homestays, as well as interesting Spanish festivals and adventures you could try out. Eating, sleeping, and relaxing are central to your stay wherever you are in the world.

More importantly, Chapter 5 provided a breakdown of the latest Covid-19 protocols and policies that need to be followed in Spain. The pandemic has affected how we socialize and how and when we can travel, and this is why we need to remain informed about any updates to traveling abroad during a pandemic. Like many countries, Spain has travel restrictions that involve testing, screening, and public laws on how people can gather and socialize. Spain's policies are necessary and are there to protect their people as well as their visitors like you. Remaining informed, alert, and conscious of the safety of you and your fellow travelers are what traveling during Covid-19 is all about.

Lastly, in Chapter 6, we learned about the many cities, towns, villages, and islands that make up the diverse Spanish landscape. We discussed what the big and bustling cities have to offer as well as the hidden villages of the coastal regions. Spanish culture is rich in history, art, food, and energy, and you can experience this unique culture anywhere you travel in and around the country. The islands of Spain also offer their own laid back, seaside lifestyle as well as outdoor adventures. The streets of Spain are iconic in the sense that you can walk along a busy street of Madrid or a cobblestone street in a remote village and still feel at home and completely immersed in Spanish culture. This guide is your introduction to life as a traveler through the hills, beaches, and city streets of Spain. Now all you need to do is take another step closer to your next Spanish adventure of 2022!

REFERENCES

10 best markets in spain. (2022). Hotels.com. https://za.hotels.com/go/spain/best-markets-spain

10 most popular streets in madrid. (2022). https://za.hotels.com/go/spain/most-popular-streets-madrid

10 top tourist attractions in spain. (2021, September 25). Touropia. https://www.touropia.com/tourist-attractions-in-spain/

23 pro tips for saving money on travel. (2022). Travel Channel. https://www.travelchannel.com/interests/budget/articles/23-pro-tips-for-saving-money-on-travel

Bennett, A. (2021, June 24). *Best of the balearics: four spanish islands to visit from the green list*. The Guardian. https://www.theguardian.com/travel/2021/jun/24/best-balaerics-spanish-islands-to-visit-green-list-mallorca-ibiza-menorca-formentera

Biggest cities in spain (top 30 by population). (2021, November 22). Mappr. https://www.mappr.co/thematic-maps/biggest-cities-spain/

Booking.com. (2022). *Cheap hotels in madrid.* Booking.com. https://www.booking.com/cheap/city/es/madrid.en-gb.html

CNN. (2022, February 9). *Traveling to spain during covid-19: what you need to know before you go.* CNN. https://edition.cnn.com/travel/article/spain-travel-covid-19/index.html

Dundas, S. (2020, November 20). *13 awe-inspiring things to do in the canary islands.* Celebrity Cruises. https://www.celebritycruises.com/blog/things-to-do-in-the-canary-islands

Fascinating Spain. (2022). *Secret spots in the major cities of spain.* Fascinating Spain. https://fascinatingspain.com/place-to-visit/the-best-of/secret-spots-in-the-major-cities-of-spain/

Fleischer, J., Junyent, M., Bac, M., Elorrieta, G., Perez, M., Santos, N., & Alamilos, A. (2022, February 8). *The 25 best things to do in spain in 2022.* Time Out. https://www.timeout.com/spain/things-to-do/best-things-to-do-in-spain

GOV.UK. (2022). *Foreign travel advice.* GOV.UK.
https://www.gov.uk/foreign-travel-advice/spain

Hamand, C. J. (2019, November 19). *27 best things to do in the balearic islands.* Travel Inspires.
https://travelinspires.org/best-things-to-do-in-the-balearic-islands/

HomeToGo. (2022). *HomeToGo Spain.* hometogo.
https://www.hometogo.com/search/5460aeae487
f8?adword=google%2Frowe%2Fkwd-
303284729678%2Fct%3Ds%3Blc%3Dst%3Bd%3Ddt
%3Btc%3DROWE%3Bln%3Den%3Bot%3DAcc%3B
lt%3Dab%3Bmt%3Db%3Bcty%3D0%3Bjm%3D1%3
Bcid%3D8114e33e115b2047%2Fes%2Fn-
a%2F5460aeae487f8%2F437890452412%2Faccommo
dations%20spain&c=USD&gclid=Cj0KCQiA3fiPBh
CCARIsAFQ8QzUYW5CtJi99DuwDlU4vGmS9Y6_
nGQRmD1n_ZBA446OOB_EN0TvFGhoaAvZQEA
Lw_wcB&hl=en_GB&mktasp=acid%3D2572727760
%3Bcpid%3D10147051678%3Bagid%3D1102105945
48%3Badid%3D437890452412%3Bdvce%3Dc%3Bk
wrd%3Daccommodations%20spain%3B

Kliger, I. (2015, October 15). *Secret streets of barcelona.*
Travel + Leisure.
https://www.travelandleisure.com/travel-
tips/offbeat/secret-streets-of-barcelona

Lloyd. (2018, June 3). *18 beautiful towns in spain to visit.* Hand Luggage Only. https://handluggageonly.co.uk/2018/06/03/18-beautiful-villages-and-towns-in-spain-to-visit/

Martucci, B. (2021, December 23). *37 ways to save money & time when traveling internationally.* Money Crashers. https://www.moneycrashers.com/international-travel-save-money-time/

Matt. (2018, April 5). *Explore charming quaint streets around spain.* Spain Guides. https://spainguides.com/destinations/travel-ideas/explore-charming-quaint-streets-around-spain/

Molly. (2020, March 14). *Delivery + take away – best food in granada spain.* Piccavey. https://www.piccavey.com/food-delivery-takeaway-granada/

Nastase, M. (2021, June 8). *The most beautiful towns in spain.* Culture Trip. https://theculturetrip.com/europe/spain/articles/the-10-most-beautiful-towns-in-spain/

Norman, L. (2021, July 30). *Best spanish experiences to bookmark for your next trip.* Six-Two. https://www.contiki.com/six-two/things-to-do-in-spain/

Ranked: The ten best markets in spain. (2022, January 10). The Local Spain. https://www.thelocal.es/20220110/ranked-the-ten-best-markets-in-spain/

Rodriguez, V. (2019). *Canary islands*. Britannica. https://www.britannica.com/place/Canary-Islands

Rogers, B. (2021, July 26). *16 top-rated tourist attractions in spain*. Planet Ware. https://www.planetware.com/tourist-attractions/spain-e.htm

Ross, P. (2015, October 8). *The best takeaways in malasaña, madrid*. Culture Trip. https://theculturetrip.com/europe/spain/articles/the-5-best-takeaways-in-malasa-a-madrid/

Spain: Camino de Santiago. (2019, April 25). Country Walkers. https://www.countrywalkers.com/tours/spain-camino-de-santiago/

The best farmers markets in spain. (2022). Inspirock. https://www.inspirock.com/farmers-markets-in-spain

The Crazy Tourist. (2015, August 13). *25 best things to do in Spain*. The Crazy Tourist.

https://www.thecrazytourist.com/top-25-things-to-do-in-spain/

The six spanish streets you just have to walk down. (2016, November 29). The Local Spain. https://www.thelocal.es/20161129/six-of-spains-most-stroll-able-streets-spain-beautiful-travel/

Things to do & must-see attractions in balearic islands. (2022). Viator. https://www.viator.com/en-ZA/Balearic-Islands/d229

Tripadvisor. (2022a). *Cheap hotels in madrid.* Tripadvisor. https://www.tripadvisor.co.za/HotelsList-Madrid-Budget-Hotels-zfp11670261.html

Tripadvisor. (2022b). *Restaurants in spain.* Tripadvisor. https://www.tripadvisor.com/Restaurants-g187427-Spain.html

yelp. (2022). *Best takeout in madrid, spain.* Yelp. https://www.yelp.com/search?find_desc=best+takeout&find_loc=Madrid&attrs=RestaurantsTakeOut&start=10

Zaino, L. (2017a, January 25). *Stroll the most beautiful streets in madrid.* Culture Trip. https://theculturetrip.com/europe/spain/articles/stroll-the-most-beautiful-streets-in-madrid/

Zaino, L. (2017b, April 10). *11 breathtaking places in spain to visit before you die*. Culture Trip. https://theculturetrip.com/europe/spain/articles/10-breathtaking-places-in-spain-to-visit-before-you-die/

Zaino, L. (2020, July 19). *15 of the most beautiful villages in spain*. The Points Guy. https://thepointsguy.com/guide/15-most-beautiful-villages-spain/

Image References

B, D. (n.d.). *White building interior photo*. [Image]. Unsplash. https://unsplash.com/photos/l6tTuz97Vcs

Gardner, A. (2017). *Bar interior view photo*. [Image]. Unsplash. https://unsplash.com/photos/NiFtfpp-AXk

JP Files. (2019). *People gathering near outdoor during daytime photo*. [Image]. Unsplash. https://unsplash.com/photos/8KhL4DAM6rk

Kurtius, M. (2021). *Brown concrete building near river during daytime photo*. [Image]. Unsplash. https://unsplash.com/photos/qwIM0ObtDCI

Norris, D. (2017). *White concrete buildings photo.*
[Image]. Unsplash.
https://unsplash.com/photos/m_B6Rq976_E

Salas, J. F. (2018). *City scale under blue sky photo.*
[Image. Unsplash.
https://unsplash.com/photos/ChSZETOal-I

Shih, Y. (2021). *Cooked shrimp on black round plate photo.*
[Image]. Unsplash.
https://unsplash.com/photos/MEW5M1WhMQE

Made in the USA
Middletown, DE
11 August 2022

71097519R00066